SandCastle™

Baby
Australian Animals

It's a Baby

Australian

Fur Seal!

Katherine Hengel

Consulting Editor, Diane Craig, M.A./Reading Specialist

ABDO
Publishing Company

Published by ABDO Publishing Company, 8000 West 78th Street, Edina, Minnesota 55439.

Printed in the United States.

Editor: Liz Salzmann
Content Developer: Nancy Tuminelly
Cover and Interior Design and Production: Kelly Doudna, Mighty Media
Photo Credits: iStockphoto.com (cbabbitt, stevenallan), Peter Arnold Inc. (Kevin Aitken, Biosphoto/Alcalay J.-J. & Marcon B., Biosphoto/Marcon Brigitte, R. Hicker, Robert J. Ross, TUNS), Shutterstock

Library of Congress Cataloging-in-Publication Data

Hengel, Katherine.
  It's a baby Australian fur seal! / Katherine Hengel.
    p. cm. -- (Baby Australian animals)
  ISBN 978-1-60453-574-7
  1. Southern fur seals--Infancy--Australia--Juvenile literature. I. Title.

QL737.P63H46 2010
599.79\738139--dc22

                                    2008055073

SandCastle™ Level: Transitional

SandCastle™ books are created by a team of professional educators, reading specialists, and content developers around five essential components—phonemic awareness, phonics, vocabulary, text comprehension, and fluency—to assist young readers as they develop reading skills and strategies and increase their general knowledge. All books are written, reviewed, and leveled for guided reading, early reading intervention, and Accelerated Reader® programs for use in shared, guided, and independent reading and writing activities to support a balanced approach to literacy instruction. The SandCastle™ series has four levels that correspond to early literacy development. The levels are provided to help teachers and parents select appropriate books for young readers.

| **Emerging Readers** | **Beginning Readers** | **Transitional Readers** | **Fluent Readers** |
| (no flags) | (1 flag) | (2 flags) | (3 flags) |

SandCastle™ would like to hear from you. Please send us your comments and suggestions.
sandcastle@abdopublishing.com

Vital Statistics

for the Australian Fur Seal

BABY NAME
pup

NUMBER IN LITTER
1

WEIGHT AT BIRTH
10 to 26 pounds (5 to 12 kg)

AGE OF INDEPENDENCE
3 to 6 years

ADULT WEIGHT
80 to 795 pounds (36 to 360 kg)

LIFE EXPECTANCY
12 to 30 years

Female Australian fur seals are called cows. They go on land to give **birth**. Australian fur seal pups are born in rocky areas.

Australian fur seals live on the **coasts** of Australia and nearby islands.

Male Australian fur seals are called bulls. They are more than twice as big as the **females**!

A group of fur seals is called a **colony**.

Cows stay with their pups for a week. Then they go out to sea to find food.

When their mothers leave, the pups stay together in groups.

9

The cows return to **nurse** their pups about once a week.

Cows nurse their pups until they are about ten months old.

11

When mother Australian
fur seals return, they
call their pups. Each pup
knows its mother's call.

After eight months, the pups can swim for several days at a time. They begin to eat some **solid** food such as fish.

Australian fur seals dive for their food. They can go as deep as 650 feet (200 m)!

Australian fur seals eat **squid,** octopus, fish, and lobster.

Great white sharks
and killer whales are
the Australian fur seal's
main **predators.**

After about five weeks,
Australian fur seal pups
shed their black fur.
They grow new, light
brown **coats**.

Fun Fact
About the Australian Fur Seal

The largest **male** Australian fur seals weigh 795 pounds (360 kg). That's about the same as 12 fourth graders!

Glossary

birth – when a person or animal is born.

coast – the land that is next to a sea or ocean.

coat – the fur covering of an animal.

colony – a group of animals or plants that live or grow together.

female – being of the sex that can produce eggs or give birth. Mothers are female.

male – being of the sex that can father offspring. Fathers are male.

nurse – to feed a baby milk from the breast.

predator – an animal that hunts others.

shed – to lose something, such as skin, leaves, or fur, through a natural process.

solid – a substance that is not a liquid or a gas.

squid – a sea animal with a soft body and ten tentacles around the mouth.

To see a complete list of SandCastle™ books and other nonfiction titles from ABDO Publishing Company, visit **www.abdopublishing.com**.

8000 West 78th Street, Edina, MN 55439

800-800-1312 • 952-831-1632 fax